Digital Painting Gui
with Procreate

The Complete Manual for Beginners with Tips and Tricks to Creating Good Art and Design on iPad Using Procreate

Christopher
Parker

Disclaimer

The information in this book is based on personal experience and anecdotal evidence. Although the author has made every attempt to achieve an accuracy of the information gathered in this book, they make no representation or warranties concerning the accuracy or completeness of the contents of this book. Your circumstances may not be suited to some illustrations in this book.

The author disclaims any liability arising directly or indirectly from the use of this book. Readers are encouraged to seek Medical. Accounting, legal, or professional help when required.

This guide is for informational purposes only, and the author does not accept any responsibilities for any liabilities resulting from the use of this information. While every attempt has been made to verify the information provided here, the author cannot assume any responsibility for errors, inaccuracies or omission.

Printed in the United States of America

Table of Contents

INTRODUCTION

If you have ever been afraid of handling digital painting applications such as Photoshop, you don't have to worry. This book proffers solutions on how to create digital drawing and painting using an Apple pencil on iPad.

Procreate is a software for various creative artworks. It is available for a one-time purchase from the App Store. You can use it with your iPad and it is also designed as Procreate Pocket for the iPhone. This app was developed by Savage Interactive and useful for digital painting.

Computer graphics can apply if for creativity, since it has active gesture control and accessible menus. Even entertainment firms, digital painters, and photographers have found it very useful for their creative designs.

CHAPTER ONE

Understanding Procreate

Procreate is a software designed for the Apple pencil and compatible with your iPad Pro. It is vital for digital art and creativity on the go. You can apply it for sketching, drawing, painting, and other visual artworks.

This advanced creative tool works with stylus tools and Apple tablets. With this tool, artists can work digitally and remotely on their smart devices. They can make designs, delete graphics, edit their work, and even share their artwork online.

How to Install the App on your iPad

If you are using an iPhone, Apple is offering a free download of the Procreate app for free from the App Store. But if you are using an iPad, you have to redeem this offer. This is probably, the first time Apple is offering a free download of an app.

Now, to install the Procreate app, ensure that you have the Apple Store app on your iPad. After this, scroll to the **Stores menu.** This is located in the lower menu bar. Navigate until you see the **iPhone Upgrade Program.**

Swipe over the app until you see the Procreate banner.

Different Ways of Using the App

As a computer graphic or illustrator, there are various ways of using Procreate in drawing and painting.

Here are the various ways of using Procreate on iPad:

a. Procreate helps you to play around with Recolor methods. You can easily customize the colors in your app to different shades. This works using Alpha Lock that maintains the lines of a particular layer. Therefore, you can use it to alter the colors in your shapes. Enable Alpha Lock and select a color from your color tab. Then, start coloring on your artwork. Any chosen color will remain within the layer and you may not color outside the lines. If you want to fill the whole layer with one color, simply, tap on the **Fill Layer button.**

Moreover, you can use Recolor feature located in the **Adjustment bar.** You will see Recolor at the lower part of the menu. The Recolor tool will fill in any color where you place the crosshairs. Changing the area where you want to paint, means that you will drag the crosshairs to such location on the screen.

b. Understanding basic gestures in Procreate. Gestures are used with your fingers like keyboard shortcuts. With these features, you can redo or undo your work by pressing two or three fingers on your canvas. If you want to clear a layer, scrub the canvas with three fingers. You can also conceal the user interface and see the entire work full-screen by pressing four fingers on the canvas.

c. Creating your own Procreate brushes. This is a better option instead of using the default brush or importing a brush from the internet. You can easily make your own.

d. Procreate uses QuickShape and QuickLine. If you cannot make straight lines, you can use these tools. As you draw a line, triangle, circle, or any other geometric shape, simply place your Apple Pencil on the window after making the shapes. Then, automatically, the app will finish the drawings perfectly for you.

e. Maintain your layers by exporting the files as PSD. Imagine whatever you want to draw on your iPad. After that send your artpiece to your PC for more editing. Then, use the export to PSD feature when you are done.

f. Procreate enables you to clip masks. This feature is similar to Alpha Lock. In this case, you will work with a new layer. You can modify your details without altering the original shape. Add a new layer and tap on clipping mask. This will cause the base layer to change to a mask. All your pixels will blend to the pixels of the original shape. But it remains separate and adjustable.

g. You can make a Color Palette with an Eyedropper tool. If you notice any image with a bright color that you can use, the eyedropper tool in Procreate will help you to save such colors directly in the app. if you want to enable eyedropper, press down the screen over the color you want to use. This will alter and blend the color dot in the top right side of your window.

h. Procreate enables you to use Alpha Lock properly. If you want to add colors, textures, and shadows to your drawings, begin by making a shape. Then, proceed to your layer menu and click on **Alpha Lock.** You can use the shortcut by swiping right with your two fingers. In this manner, if you add any content it will be confined within the layers. This will prevent you from coloring outside your original shape.

i. Using Blend modes to design new layers. With Procreate app, you can cover the content of a layer properly. This will help to blend the colors, textures, and shapes of various layers well. This is located in the **Layers menu.**

Look at the right side of each layer, you will see letter N. This entails **Normal mode.** It is the default **Blend Mode setting.** Open the Blend Modes setting by tapping on **Letter N.** it has options that will enable you to brighten, darken, and control layer opacity.

Advantages of Using Procreate

Here are the various benefits of using Procreate:

1. You can easily arrange your designs in a form of gallery.
2. You can import files from different locations and devices.
3. Procreate enables you to zoom in and out of your artwork.
4. Easy to integrate with your regular workflows.
5. Ability to navigate through other platforms and apps seamlessly.
6. It is a top-notch professional tool for computer graphics.
7. Ability to undo changes to your creativities.
8. Easy to adjust layers by creating and developing your artworks at an increasing speed.

How to Use Apple Pencil in Procreate

Apple pencil will help you to access the full potentials of Apple pencil including its speed and efficiency. There are supported brushes that could be used with the tip of this pencil.

Setting up Apple pencil

You should set up this pencil before using it. Simply, pair it with your iPad. After pairing it begin to draw immediately. There is no need to connect the pencil to Procreate. It operates naturally with the tip and pressure from the pencil.

You can use the brush responses the way they are designed or customize them to fit your artwork.

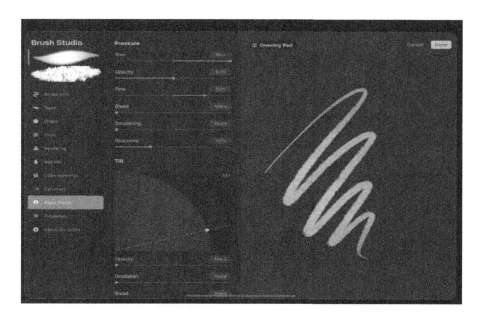

The type of pressure you apply to Apple pencil determines the response from the brushes. Also, the size of the brush depends on the pressure from Apple pencil. You will form thicker strokes by pressing harder on the pencil.

The opacity of the image depends on the tip of the brush. If you hold your brush upright, you will get a solid line. But it can fade, when you tilt the pencil. You can switch between two textures of the brush.

You can also have distinct effects by blending Apple pencil with Procreate brushes. There are numerous customizable settings at your disposal.

Another way is by exploring the brush studio settings to discover the different ways Procreate brushes and Apple pencil functions.

Navigating the Procreate Interface

With Procreate, you can handle your projects quickly using multi-touch gestures. You will be able to manage the interface with less and tools with less effort.

Some of the ways to explore the interface includes

1. Using the Interface – the interface has three features that can help you in handling your artwork professionally. These include customize interface, dark or light interface, and hide interface.

Moreover, the interface has some painting tools for effective creativity and designs. They are located on the right menu bar numbered 1 – 5, the sidebar numbered 6 – 9, and the advanced features numbered 10 – 14.

The Customize Interface

You can customize the interface on your Procreate window to modify it to your satisfaction.

Light or Dark Interface

There are double visual modes on the interface, which are light mode or dark mode. The light mode involves a higher contrast and ideal for working in bright settings. The dark mode is an unobtrusive charcoal interface that concentrates on your artwork.

If you decide to change to light mode, press **Actions** and select **Prefs**. Then, tap on **Light Interface**.

Hide Interface

This interface enables you to handle your artwork with minimal distractions using only a brush. This will help you to view your project properly with maximum concentration.

With this, you can see your canvas properly since the interface will slide away. You can restore the interface by moving to the upper left side and pressing the Full Screen indicator. Another way is by hitting on the screen with four fingers.

You can also use gestures to restore the most common tools if your interface is concealed in Full-Screen mode.

Other features on the interface include:

The Left or Right sidebar

When you are painting with your right hand, the sidebar will be accessible to your left hand. The interface on your right-hand is designed for those who like it on that side of the canvas. Simply, hit on **Actions** and choose **Prefs**. Then, click on **right-hand interface** to change sides.

The Brush Cursor

Before using this feature, it is good to examine the shape of your brush. After activating the Brush cursor, the shape of the brush will be displayed whenever, you want to use it on the canvas. With this, you can view and access the shape of the mark, you are making.

Therefore, click on **Actions** and select **Prefs** from the bar. Then, tap on the **Brush cursor** to enable or disable it.

The movable side bar

You can customize the height of your sidebar on Procreates interface.

Go to the edge of the interface and drag a finger over the **Modify icon.** This will cause the sidebar to slide out from the side of the canvas. Now, pull it up or down before placing it on a comfortable position for you. This is functional on the right-hand or left-hand interface modes.

CHAPTER TWO

Overview of the Procreate Gallery

The Procreate gallery is designed to enable you create the perfect canvas for your project. You should arrange your gallery the way you want it. But Procreate will store your art creations in a pleasant manner. Here, you will discover how to import images and share your creations with your loved ones.

Here are some steps to use the gallery:

a. Create your designs using different preset canvasses. You can also set up a custom canvas for your work. Press the Plus sign at the upper right side of the gallery to select a new canvas window.

b. Preview your artworks in full-screen. This includes animations and other creative designs you have by flipping through your creations in a collection. You can view all your projects without leaving the gallery.

c. Use Procreate's gallery to organize your workspace. Speed your workflow and manage your space using Stacks.

d. You can import an image for a new canvas. Then, you will share your creativity with your contacts.

e. Procreates gallery helps you to import and export various projects with different file formats. Your project saves as .procreate file format. However, some other supported files include .GIF, .PNG, .PSD, .JPEG, and .TIFF.

What are the Painting Tools Required in Procreate?

The necessary painting tools for your artwork in Procreate are located on different sections of the interface such as the upper right menu bar, left side bar, and advanced features found at the upper left side of the window.

Note: The numbers on the screen represent various tools, which I have explained below.

Some of these tools include

a. **Tools at the Upper Right Menu** – these are referred to as the beginning tools for your creativity on Procreate. They include painting, smudging, erasing, making layers, and coloring.

1. Painting tool – the painting tool involves smooth and flexible brushes that you can use for sketching, inking, and painting your artwork. You can customize your brushes, organize them in a library, or import custom brushes.

2. Smudging tool – helps you to add various effects by blending your artwork and mixing the colors.

3. Erasing tool – useful for correcting errors and making adjustments. Go to the Brush library to pair your eraser to the type of creativity you are making.

4. Tool for making layers – enables you to shift, edit, recolor, and remove peculiar elements. You can color overlapping objects without destroying your artwork.

5. Coloring tool - this is used for choosing, adjusting, and blending the colors in your design. You can drag and drop colors inside your art. You can also save, import, and share palettes.

The Features on the Left Side of Your App

The tools available on the left side bar will help you in adjusting the sizes of brush and the opacity of your artwork. You can also modify, redo, and undo your creativity by pressing the related buttons on the window.

6. Tool for Increasing the Size of Brush – used for increasing the tip of the brush for a thicker mark by dragging the top slider up. You can drag it down for a thinner mark. If you want to adjust your drawing, click any

point on the slider to skip to that point. Hold the slider and drag your finger sideways without lifting the finger to get a desirable stroke. You can pull the slider up or down for smaller increments.

7. Modify tool – this tool will help you to select colors from the sidebar using the eyedropper feature. Simply, slide the eyedropper over the color you want to select and release your hand to pick it. Another way is to press down the Modify tool and press anywhere to choose a color using the eyedropper. The Modify icon could be used in prompting other tools in the system. Therefore, you can design your own customized shortcuts.

Customized Actions

8. Tool for Brush opacity – you can reduce or increase the opacity of your brush from transparent to solid by dragging the lower slider up or down. If you want to experience more changes in the degree of opacity, press the slider and pull your finger sideways. Drag the slider up or down without lifting your finger and you will see smaller increments in the appearance of the image.

9. Undo or Redo tools – this is used for doing or redoing the last thing you did. You can redo or undo up to two hundred and fifty

actions on the app. If you want to redo any action, click on the lower arrow. There will be a notification on the interface to allow you understand the action to undo or redo. Also, you can press down both arrows to undo or redo multiple actions quickly.

Using the Advanced Features in Procreate or left side bar

The tools within this menu is designed to enable you undertake complex adjustment to your designs.

10. Gallery tool – if you want to arrange and manage all your artworks. You can allow others to view your creations by sharing it to them from the gallery menu. Also, you can import images and create new canvasses as you like.

11. Action tool – this tool is designed to enable you handle all practical features on the app. you can insert, share, and adjust your canvas including other elements

inside. If you want to encounter more unique features in your workflow, this tool is available for you. Also, you can customize your touch settings and adjust the interface for productivity and efficiency.

12.   Adjustment tool – this can help you to make professional finishing effects to your creations using imagery features in the Adjustment window. You can handle gradient mapping and make complex color adjustments quickly. You can apply the power of Liquify to handle adjustments to your artwork in the system. Other features useful for this creativity include Clone, Sharpen, Blur, and Noise. Some other exclusive effects to boost your art piece include chromatic aberration, bloom, halftone, and glitch.

13.   Selection tool – there are four flexible selection features that can help you to separate any part of your image for improvement. You will also find other

advanced options to enable you control your customization processes in Procreate.

14.   Transform tool – in the event that you want to carry out faster editions; you can use the transform tool to shift, stretch, and manipulate your images. You can use it customize and manipulate your images. It helps you to undertake simple scaling and flexible warp meshing.

How to Create a New Project

If you want to create a new project, simply set up a custom canvas or pick from different preset canvasses. Tap on the Plus icon (+) at the top right of the screen. This will prompt up the **New canvas window.**

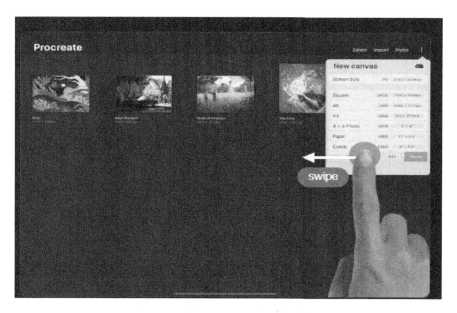

You can enjoy faster and easier creation using preset templates. Select the templates according to the various sizes that will be useful for the type of creation you want to make. The various sizes include square, A4 paper, screen size, high-resolution 4K, and square. Others include US paper and 4 x 6 photo.

After your selection, you can swipe left or right to delete or preset your canvas. Scroll and click on the Edit icon to use the interface of a custom canvas.

You can modify the features of the canvas and know the highest number of layers available in it.

How to Customize the Interface

You can decide to customize the interface if the preset sizes are not working. In this case, you can create or edit your own canvas to fit your purpose.

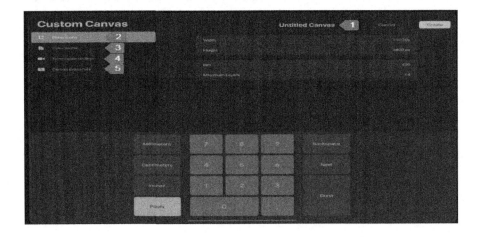

Go to the app window and click on the **Plus (+) button** to invoke the **New Canvas screen.** This involves rectangle with a Plus sign at the upper right edge of the screen.

You can modify your canvas using the Name, Dimensions, Color profile, Time-lapse settings, and canvas properties.

a. Edit the Name of the Canvas – you can call up the keyboard by clicking on **Untitled canvas** at the upper part of the window. Change the name by entering a new name for your custom canvas preset. Then, select Return to commit. Another method is writing with your Apple Pencil.

b. Change the Dimensions of the Canvas – these include the height, width, and DPI of your new preset canvas. Simply, click on the value you want to adjust. This will prompt up a number keyboard. Enter the size you want in the number key below.

If you alter the size of the canvas, the number of layers will be affected. But larger canvasses will give you fewer layers while smaller canvasses give more layers.

You can set the size of your canvas in pixels, millimeters, inches, or centimeters. If you want to alter the unit of measurement for your canvas, use the buttons on the keyboard at the lower part of the left side of your window. But this depends on the model of your iPad. You can have pixels as large as 16 K or as small as 1 x 1 pixels.

c. Manage the color using color profiles – this is one of the ways to handle color settings. RGB is the best color profile for displaying artwork on your windows. It handles color by seeing it as a blend of red, green, and blue.

On the other hand, if you want to print your artwork, you can use CMYK. This entails a blend of cyan, magenta, yellow, and black. This is evidenced in commercial printing. You can select the right color space by knowing the right destination of your artwork. With this, you will have the most vivid and proper color results.

Another method is to use the default setting if you don't know the color space to use. Therefore, there are seventeen color profiles within Procreate to give you the best creative experience. Most artists prefer the default profile such as Display P3 and Generic CMYK profile.

d. Enter New Time-lapse settings for your creation – the app can record your progress while you create and design your artwork. You can do a replay of your progress in artwork creativity as a time-lapse video. With this, every canvas you are creating on the interface will have a time-lapse setting. Simply, choose the resolution of your video. This could be from 1080p to full 4K resolution. Also, you can adjust the settings of the quality of your recordings from Low to Lossless. The Low is suitable for sharing since it is a smaller file size. Moreover, the Lossless is larger in size and comes in a superior quality with no loss of details.

You can also use HEVC, which entails a new form of video compression for superior motion films. You can export the video file and it is smaller in size with greater quality.

You will see this feature in programming, green-screening, web integration, and video overlays. HEVC permits you to use a transparent background in your videos. Set your canvas color profile to sRGB IEC61966-2.1, if you want to export a time-lapse video with a transparent background. Then, toggle on HEVC.

e. Handle the Features of the Canvas – you can choose a default background color for your artwork and canvas preset. You may also decide to hide the background.

Using the Sidebar of iPad Pro

To use the sidebar of your iPad Pro means to extend your workspace and use the iPad as a second display for your projects. With this, you can use the same app on both screens. For instance, you can see your artwork on the screen of a Mac device as you use Apple Pencil including an app's palettes and tools on iPad.

Therefore, the sidebar will allow you use the same app on both screens. Now, to use the side bar on iPad, press the buttons on the side bar. This will reveal the menu bar or hide it. You can also tap the **Dock** and **keyboard.**

Another way is pressing one or more modifier buttons like the CTRL if you want to use keyboard.

CHAPTER THREE

How to Create a New Project on

Procreate

As I said earlier, if you want to create a new project on Procreate, you should pick from various preset canvasses. You can also set up a custom canvas for your artwork.

Click on the Plus sign at the upper right side of the gallery. This will give you a new canvas to work on.

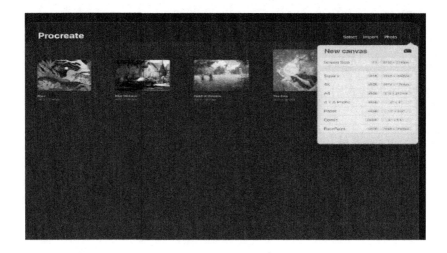

These templates are available in different sizes. Simply, select the one you want to use and begin to create your designs using Apple Pencil.

Using Gestures

With gestures, you can manage your art creation potentials. There are three types of gestures such as basic gestures, layer gestures, and customize gestures.

Applying basic gestures in Procreate

This will cause you to move around your canvas. You can clear, copy, paste, and discover valuable menus easily. Again, you can use the **Undo or Redo buttons** properly.

Here are different basic gestures to use in your creativities:

1. Press the **Erase tool** including smudge and paint on your canvas to start working on your

new project. In this case, you don't need an Apple Pencil to create your designs. Simply, apply your fingertips.

2. Zoom in and out of your art designs using a pinch of your fingers. This will cause you to move from beautiful details to a finer picture. Position your fingers on the canvas. Then, you can zoom out by pinching your fingers together. But if you want to zoom in, pinch your fingers apart from each other.

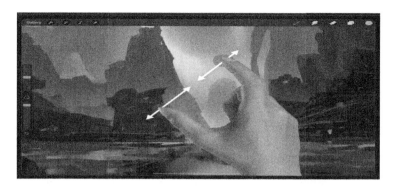

3. Rotate your Art design to a desirable angle using pinch to twist. As you pinch on the canvas, rotate your fingers. This will cause the canvas to turn.

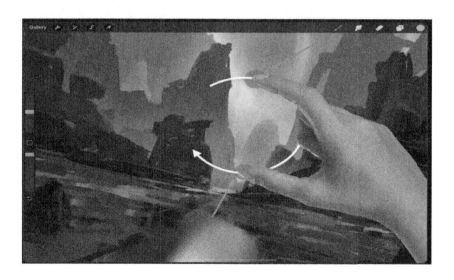

4. Easily fit your canvas to the window using a quick pinch action. This action is carried out much faster causing the canvas to open in full size on the interface. After the action, simply lift up your fingers.

5. Press the canvas with two fingers to undo an action. You can position your fingers together or separate. After doing this, you will see a notification on the window informing you the action you want to undo. The app can undo up to two hundred and fifty actions in your system. Remove your fingers from the screen to stop it.

6. Using a three finger touch permits you to carry out a Redo action on your projects. You may position your fingers together or separate. Also, if you want to redo a series of actions, press three fingers on your canvas.

7. To clear a layer instantly, use three-finger scrub. Move your three fingers from one side to another in a scrubbing action.

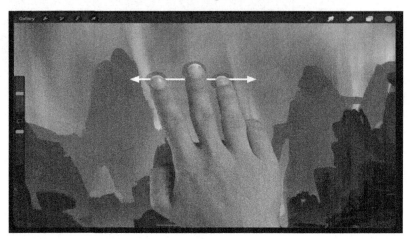

8. Cut, copy, and paste using three-finger swipe. Use a floating menu with the copy, cut, and paste methods. Simply, swipe three fingers down the screen to prompt the copy and paste menu. You can also use the copy, cut, copy All, Duplicate, paste, and cut & paste.

9. Press four fingers on the screen for full-screen display. With this, you can work on your art using a brush and minimal distractions. Press four fingers on the screen whenever you want to work without any boundary.

   This will produce a Full-screen mode and the border will shift to give you a better glance of the canvas. If you want to reverse the interface, press your four fingers on the screen again. Another method is by pressing the Full Screen indicator at the upper left side.

10.   Using QuickShape to perfect your artwork by drawing and holding it. You should draw a line or shape and position your finger on the canvas. You can also place the stylus on the canvas too.

This action will turn your stroke into a closest detected figure or straight line. As you press down your finger, use another finger to tap on the complete version of that shape.

11.   Accurate slider control. In Procreate, sliders provide better control while drawing. Remove your fingers from the sidebar and hold the slider. Then, pull them up and down to adjust in smaller increments.

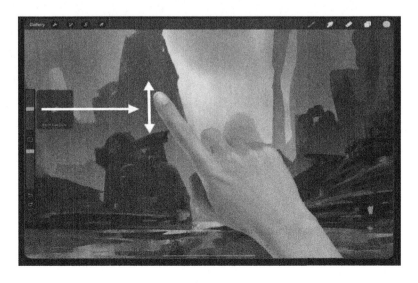

Using Layer Gestures in Procreate

This enables you to function better in the layers panel with these simple gestures.

12.   Blending two or more layers into one using pinch to merge. Simply, pinch two layers together and merge them.

13.   Choose a primary layer by taping on the Layers panel. This will activate the layer making it to change to a bright blue color. It

will also become your primary layer. Every design you perform in Procreate affects this layer.

14.   Pick a Secondary Layer by Swiping Right. Go to the **Layers panel** and swipe right to add it to your selection as a secondary layer. These layers are displayed in dark blue. You can have several secondary layers with only a primary layer at a time. Every design or drawing you make will show on the primary layer.

15.   Modify the opacity of your layer using a two-finger tap. Initiate opacity controls on a layer by pressing on it with your two fingers. With this, it becomes the primary layer. Reduce or increase the transparency of the layer by moving left or right on your canvas. Make a selection and press the layer with your two fingers to adjust the opacity. You will see changes inside the chosen area.

16.   Initiate Alpha Lock using a two-finger
swipe. This will enable you to lock the content
and transparency of the layer. Go to the
Layers menu and swipe a layer from left to
right using two fingers. After this, any
subsequent drawings or designs will only be
seen on the existing artwork on the layer.
Other transparent areas will be like a mask
and stay untouched. Also, you will not be able
to use shading elements and texture outside
the lines.

17.   Select the contents of a layer using a two-finger hold. Move to the Layers menu. Tap and hold a layer using two fingers. This will highlight the sections where you have painted or pasted your designs. The areas that are not transparent will not be selected. You can perform different actions on the highlighted section like copying, clearing, painting, and transforming it.

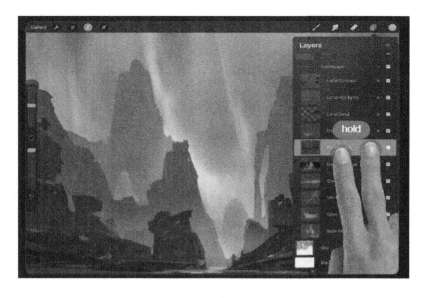

Using Customize Gestures in Procreate

18.   Maintain your workflow by changing your gestures and making your own shortcuts. With this, you can modify the shortcuts for different tools within Procreate. Click on **Actions** and select **Prefs.** Then, tap on Gesture Controls to launch the **Gesture Controls menu.**

In some cases, some shortcuts will be toggled ON or OFF. Also, you can set up multiple shortcuts with the same function. If you are not using most functions, simply deactivate them. In some cases, some shortcuts are triggered by press and hold using the slider. You cannot assign the same shortcut to two different features. If there are conflicting shortcuts, a warning icon with yellow color will be displayed on the screen beside the conflicting menu.

Managing the Color Menu

If you want to create your artpiece using color profiles that will enable you to achieve a better result on the screen or in print, use color profiles. Select from CMYK list, P3 wide color, and Procreates native sRGB. Another way is importing your personal color profiles.

However, printers and screens are different in how they handle colors. But color profiles can make your artworks outstanding.

To access Color profiles, scroll to the Procreate gallery and click on the **Plus icon** at the upper right side to display the **New Canvas menu.**

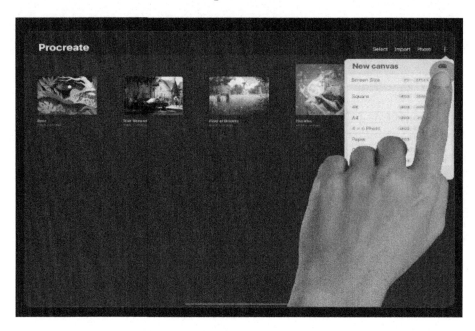

Click on the rectangle with the **Plus button** at the upper right corner and select **Custom canvas interface.**

Here are different ways to manage color menu:

1. Using RGB or CMYK

   RGB is made for art designs to be viewed on your screens. It analyzes each color as red, green, and blue. However, CMYK is the best alternative for artpieces created to be printed. In this case, colors could be analyzed as cyan, magenta, yellow, and black.

2. Changing Color Profiles

If you set your color profile with CMYK or RGB profile, you can change it any time. Simply, click on **Actions** and select **Canvas button.** From the options, press on **Canvas Information** and tap on **Color Profile.** Here, you can select the profile you want to change.

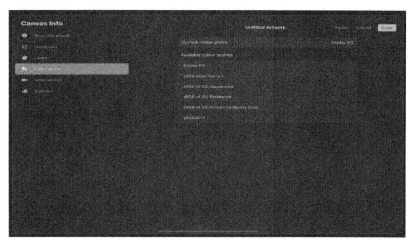

3. Importing Color Profiles

You can customize your color profiles or download them by clicking on the Import button to add these to Procreate.

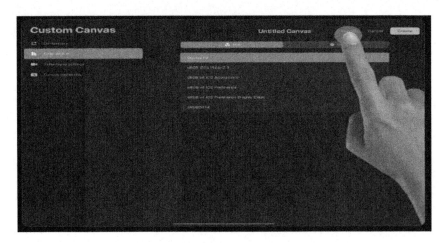

Applying Colors

If you are adjusting the colors in your artwork, there are several interface options that can help you in choosing and harmonizing the colors. This will also define your workflow. Simply pull and drop the color into your art. Then, save it or import and share the palettes. Also, Harmony can suggest complimentary colors that can fit the mood of your piece.

Other ways to apply colors to your work are through interface, disc, classic, profiles, harmony, value, and palettes.

a. The Interface helps you to select, save, and adjust your colors in the color panel

The significance of the figures 1 = color icon, 2 = Active color, 3 = Secondary color, 4 = History, 5 = Default palette, and 6 = Color Disc.

.

b. The Disc is designed to help you in selecting the accurate color and shade to handle color saturation. Go to the right side of the upper menu and choose the Color icon. Press on it and launch the Color panel. You will see the Procreate's color disc displayed by default.

c. The Classic section offers a natural way to pick colors. It involves hue, brightness, and saturation sliders. Tap the **Color icon** on the right side of the menu. This will launch the **color Picker**. Press the Classic button at the lower edge of the window.

The figures represent 1 = Classic color, 2 = hue, saturation, and brightness sliders. While 3 = Finishing up bar.

d. Harmony section uses your selections to organize automatic color schemes such as analogous, triadic, tetradic, complementary, and split complementary.

Go to the upper right side of the menu and choose the **Color icon**. Press on it and open the Control panel. Now, select the **Harmony icon.**

The figures represent: 1 = Saturation or Hue disc, 2 = Brightness slider

e. The Value section helps you to reproduce colors with the precision sliders. It is used for handling hexadecimal numerical inputs, red, green, blue, hue, saturation, and brightness.

The figures represent 1 = hue / brightness / saturation, red / green / blue, hexadecimal, and finishing up.

f. The palettes section helps you in storing your palettes section as swatches. You can also make and import cool palettes to the platform. This will make your preferred color scheme automatic.

How to Handle the Brushes

Procreates brushes are used for sketching, inking, painting, smudging, and erasing your artworks. It helps you to design calligraphy and paint using great textures. You can also organize and store your brushes, import, and store new ones in the app.

Here are various ways to handle brushes:

1. Paint, smudge, and erase buttons are used for creating different designs with your fingers or Apple pencil.

These tools could be seen at the upper right of the interface. They are represented by 1 =

paint, 2= Smudge, and 3 = Erase. All these icons are within the Brush library.

Press any button representing the feature you want to use. If you want to paint, use the brush button. This is used for adding colors to your canvas. Click on the brush icon and choose from the Brush Library. Then, make marks by dragging your finger along the canvas.

Also, if you want to smudge, then, apply the finger button. The smudge is used for blending your artwork and smoothing strokes. You can also use it for mixing colors. It is used for moving colors around your canvas.

Finally, if you want to erase any mistake, apply the Eraser.

2. Brush library – is designed for arranging, editing, sharing, and exploring the wealth of different brushes in the Procreate system. There are several brushes organized into themed categories. This gives you unimaginable scope of artistic creativities.

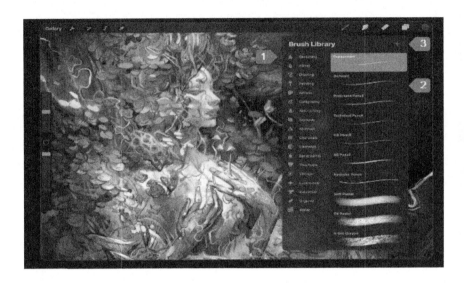

3. Brush Studio – the interface of the brush studio is divided into three sections such as drawing pad, settings, and attributes.

Drawing Pad - this is where you can preview your brush and view the changes you have made inside the brush studio. It is like a notepad that you can use in testing the color of your brushes.

Settings – use sliders, simple controls, and toggles to adjust the settings in each category.

Attributes – there are eleven attributes of the brush that could be adjusted using various settings. These features are located in the left side menu of the system. Here, you can customize the shape and grain of your brush. Also, you can change the stroke path and the way Procreate generates the final outcome.

4. Brush studio settings

Press the features on the left-hand menu, if you want to change any settings. There are some adjustable settings in the brush studio such as:

a. The stroke path – useful for plotting several points on the path made by your Apple pencil or finger.

b. The taper – for adjusting the thickness and opacity of your brushes. This occurs at the beginning or end of your brushes.

c. Shape – transfer an image into the shape source by adjusting the rotation, frequency, scatter, including the properties of the shape.

d. The grain – make a new grain from an image using the grain editor. You can set up the grain to move with the stroke or remain behind it.

e. The process of rendering the brush to the screen. Move under the hood to adjust render modes. Edit the manner colors and strokes respond to your brush as it touches the canvas.

f. Using brush properties - you can alter the way the preview of your brush is shown in the library. You will see the way the brush inclines to your screen rotation. Then, set default smudge strength.

g. Using wet mix enables you to change the way the brush relates with color. You will also know how the color interacts with the canvas. Use water to dilute the color on the brush. Begin with much paint on the brush or a little. Allow the pigment to bleed into other colors and pull them around.

h. Apply color dynamics – apply your brush to change color, saturation, and brightness based on the pressure and angle of your Apple Pencil.

i. Using Apple Pencil – customize how your Apple pencil interacts with the brush. This will affect the basic behaviors of the brush in areas such as size, bleed, flow, and opacity.

5. Dual brush – you can combine brushes by selecting, combining, editing, and blending them. You can also uncombine the brushes.

With this, you can apply the editable features including the brush's grain to make a new brush for your artworks.

Open the **Brush library** by clicking on the Brush button. You will see two brushes to combine. Tap on the first (Primary) brush and select it. It will change to blue. Pick a secondary brush by swiping on the screen and it will turn dark blue. Then, you will see the word **Combine** at the upper side of the window. Click on it to join the brushes.

6. Import and share your brushes using Adobe® Photoshop®. ABR and Procreate brush. You can add them to your brush library using In-app Import and File Association.

After importing the brushes, you can share them using the process of drag and drop

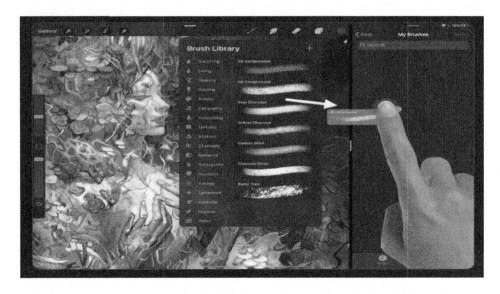

Operating the Quick Menu

The Quick menu is designed for convenience and one-touch flexibility. You can activate, invoke, or customize it. This menu provides customizable radial options that can help you n working faster and better.

The six buttons on the Quick menu are customizable. These include the radial icons and the shortcuts.

If you want to enable Quick menu, follow these processes:

Click on the **Actions icon** and select **Prefs.** Press on **Gesture controls.** From the options, **tap on Quick menu,** then toggle a shortcut to activate it.

You can also use **Touch** to enable Quick menu if you decide to use **Apple pencil.**

Managing the Screen Sizes

The screen sizes include various templates for making a new project canvas better. Some of the screen sizes include screen size, square, high-resolution 4K, US paper, 4 x 6 photo, and A4 paper.

CHAPTER FOUR

How to Navigate the Actions Menu

With the Actions menu, you will maintain perfect control of your work and customize the interface the way you want it. You can manage every aspect of the app from the **Settings menu** to the **Sharing menu**.

The Actions menu helps you to access the settings of your tools including interface appearance. Also, it is useful for handling core controls in the system.

Scroll to the menu bar on the upper part of the screen and click on the **Wrench symbol.** It is the Actions button. Pressing it will launch the **Actions menu.**

You can add pictures, texts, and share photos including layers on the app. Other features to add in the app include recording of time-lapsed video, customizing your interface including touch controls, and navigating relevant information and links.

Adding Texts and Photos

If you want to bring creativity into your artwork, simply add files, texts, and images into your canvas. This could be done by cutting, copying, and pasting relevant files of the work into the system. Also, you can copy the whole canvas into the app.

Here are ways to add texts inside your Procreate app:

Enter editable vector texts into your document to make striking art word and snappy designs.

You can use the typography tools in Procreate to design your artworks professionally. Produce crisp vector text with great editing features. There are several preloaded fonts that you can use. Also, you can import your own favorites.

Now, press the **Wrench button** in the upper left of the window. This will open the **Actions menu**. Simply, click on the **Add icon** and select **Add text.** Then, a text box will appear on the canvas. You can move it to any location on the screen and start typing.

If you want to change the color of the words, press on the **Color button.** You can also click on the **Edit Style icon.** This will give you access to various fonts, editing options, and design tools.

If you are satisfied with the outcome of your text, then scroll to the **Layers panel.** Then, click on the thumbnail of your Text layer and select **Rasterize.** This converts your vector text to pixels and applies the attributes of Procreate to it.

Here are ways to add photos to your Procreate:

The figures represent 1 = Insert a file, 2 = Insert an image, and 3 = Take a picture.

1. Insert a File – if your device is connected, go to the **Files app** and insert a photo. Press **Actions button** and choose the **Add icon.** Then, tap on **Insert a File** from the lists.

    This action will open the Files app to show your recent pictures. Another way is to use the navigation bar at the lower part to search for all linked folders and images. Supported files include PSD, JPEG, and PNG. However, PSD files added in this way will appear as a flattened image. But you can use Gallery import if you want to have a PSD file with all layers intact.

2. Insert an Image – you can add an image into your canvas using the Photos app. Simply, press on the **Actions menu** and click on **Add** from the list. Then, select **Insert Photo** from the popup tab. This will display the Photos app. Go through the folders to locate pictures that you have captured and saved images in your device.

3. Take a Picture - you can take a photo with your device and add it into your canvas. Click on the **Actions menu.** From the options, select Add and then press **Take a picture.** This will activate the built-in camera.

   Now, to take a photo, click on Use Photo and it will be displayed in any open document available for use.

On the other hand, some images may not appear in your gallery, if they are imported as a Private

Layer. Files could be added from a connected device as a Private layer using the **Files app.**

Customizing the Canvas

You can initiate changes to your canvas from a menu. Features such as Animation assist, crop, drawing guides, including resize and flip can help you in customizing your canvas. Also, detailed information about your artwork is available on the canvas.

One of the ways to customize the canvas is by using crop and resize feature.

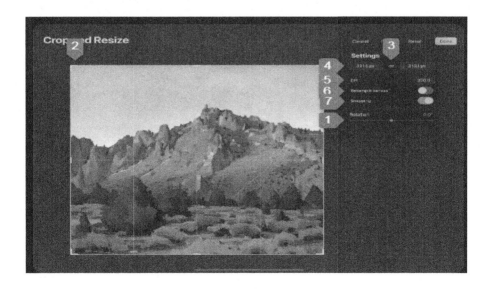

If you want to change the size and shape of your canvas to a better format, you should use the crop and resize tool.

Scroll and press on the **Actions section**. From the popup menu, select **Canvas** and tap on the **Crop and Resize area.** This action will cause the Crop and resize aspect to be displayed as a grid overlay on your image. Your canvas will adopt some new edges. But you can adjust it in different ways such as:

a. Rotate – enables you to rotate your artwork in a different angle. The slider is in the lower toolbar and will help you to adjust your canvas to the desirable crop area.

b. Freeform crop – increase or crop the size of your canvas by dragging the edges of the grid overlay. Stretch the size of your canvas on an axis by pulling one side of the overlay. Also, drag a corner point by adjusting the size of the canvas on either horizontal or vertical axis.

c. Uniform cropping – to do this, you have to lock your aspect ratio. It will also help you to enlarge the canvas.

d. Numerical cropping – use numerical sizes to enlarge or crop your canvas properly. In the lower toolbar, you will have numerical readouts showing the height and width of your canvas.

e. Adjust the Dots Per Inch (DPI) of your image on the canvas. Press **Actions** and select **Canvas**. Then, tap on **Crop and Resize** before entering the desired DPI. This indicates how many pixels are in the canvas.

f. Use resampling to scale your picture up or down. Click on the **Actions button** and choose **Canvas**. From the popup menu, tap on **Crop and Resize.** Toggle on the Resampling icon to start resizing your files.

g. Using crop and resize to snap – this can happen if you press **Actions menu** and select **Canvas tab.** Then, click on **Crop and Resize** from the popup window. In this case, the corners of the grid overlay will snap to the edges of your art designs inside the canvas instantly.

Using Animation Assistant

The animation assist is an interface within Procreate that enables you to design great motion graphics including animations.

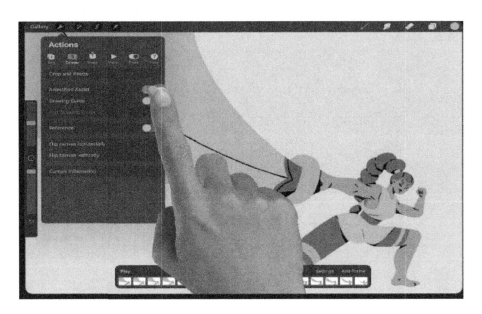

This app will assist you to recreate and refresh your app. There is a visual timeline of your animation. This also include onion-skinning that will help you get directions using **Play and Pause controls.**

It provides better options for you to handle your motion pictures. Press the Wrench icon in the upper left side of the window. This will open the **Actions menu.** Click on Canvas to turn over the **Animation Assist icon.**

With this, the **Animation Assist** will be enabled.

Handling the Pressure Curve

If you want to customize the appearance of the interface of your canvas to a connected screen, you can use Procreate and maintain your workflow. You can also change the pressure curve and link a third-party stylus. Another way is personalizing the gesture controls to fit your preferences.

Now, to edit and manage the pressure curve, it is necessary to match the stylus sensitivity to the way you create your designs. There is a better dynamic range in the Apple Pencil.

If you apply the Apple pencil with a lighter touch, you may not get the full benefits of this feature in the default settings. You have to press it down harder to get maximum opacity. Due to this discrepancy, it is advisable to use the customizable feature of the pressure curve in Procreate. In this way, you can adjust the stylus and feel of your Apple Pencil the way you want.

Simply, click on **Edit Pressure Curve** on the screen. This will launch the **Pressure curve panel.** You will see the default curve, which is a straight diagonal line. Pull this line curve to move it as a smooth curve.

The horizontal axis of the chart expresses pressure while the vertical axis is used to set up the values of the output of your pencil.

CHAPTER FIVE

How to Reference Your Work in

Procreate

This feature is designed to enable you maintain your line work, especially if you want to color on a different layer. It is suitable for artists that want to make line drawings. It is also useful for faster coloring process. On the other hand, illustrators, cartoonists, and graphic artists can find this tool helpful in their creativities.

The Purpose of Referencing your Work

a. To change the color of a shape easily.

b. Sets the mood and speeds up your coloring process without hassles.

c. Transfers colors to a different layer without affecting the initial line art.

How it Works

a. Make a line art or drawing.

b. Tap on the layer of the line art.

c. A menu will pop-up, then select **Reference.**

d. Design a new layer on top or below the reference layer.

e. Apply the select tool to choose a particular area or multiple areas of the line drawing.

f. You can use a brush for textured effect or drag and drop to fill the color instantly.

g. After this, change your layer from Reference back to regular. Simply, click and choose the reference icon a second time.

h. You can make the second layer a reference layer if you multiple line art layers for different parts of your artwork.

Making a New Canvas

To make a new canvas, you can select from various preset canvasses. Also, you can set up a **Custom canvas** for your designs.

Locate the Plus icon (+) on your canvas at the upper right side of the gallery. This will prompt the **New Canvas menu.**

Organizing the Canvas

If you want to organize your canvas, you can use the Gallery in Procreate. Also, Stacks is made to organize your workflow and keep your artwork neat.

Here are different ways to organize your artwork on Procreate:

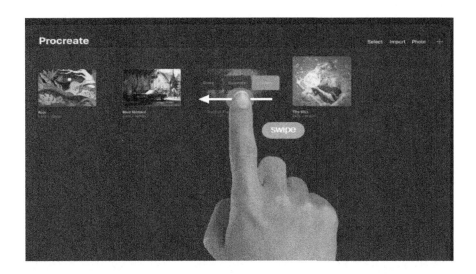

Swipe the thumbnail of your artwork to the left side. This will display some actions. However, you will see options that will prompt you to share, duplicate, and delete the artwork.

You can also rearrange your art designs by pressing on the thumbnail to lift it out of the grid. Then, drag it to a choice location and drop it.

Another way to organize your gallery is to apply bulk actions. This will save you time as you can easily share, delete, or duplicate a canvas at the same time.

Now, press the **Select icon** to enter multiple selection modes. Click on Canvasses to choose them and they will change to a blue tick. After selecting all the artworks you want, you can use the toolbar icons to Share, Duplicate, and Delete whatever item you want.

To rearrange selected Stacks and artworks in your gallery, press down the artwork to highlight and pick all of them up. Pull them to a desired location in the Gallery and drop them.

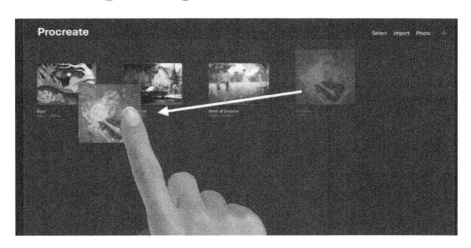

How to Share your Artwork

To share your artwork, you need to export layers from one artwork to a page with several PDFs, PNGs, MP4, and animated GIFs.

Press on the **Actions menu** and select **Share.** Scroll to the **Share layers area** of the **Share menu** and click on the **Layer export formats menu.** Every format there will apply your layers in a unique way.

How to Flip the Canvas

You can flip the canvas and rotate your artwork after designing it. With this, you can preview the canvas in sideways and upside down positions. Press two fingers on the thumbnail and rotate it until the artwork is straight upward.

Using the Data from the Canvas

The data on your canvas include images, pictures, and texts. These could be shared in various formats such as the PNG, PSD, PDF, JPEG, and TIFF.

How to Share Photos

You can share your creative art designs as a native. procreate file. It can also be a layered Adobe®Photoshop® PSD. The files could be exported as a practical PDF, JPEG, PNG, and TIFF.

Here are different ways of sharing photos and images through Procreate in your iPad device:

1. Using native .procreate format to share your files. Simply, click on the **Actions tab** and press

the **Share button.** From the options, click on Procreate and choose a storage location for your files. This format helps in preserving your artwork in the original data that you created them.

2. Using PSD to share your photos in Procreate. You can export your artwork in the file format of Adobe® Photoshop®. Click on the **Actions tab** and select the **Share button** from the list. Then, click on **PSD icon.** After this, choose a storage location for your pictures. It can store your image as the standard format preferred by Adobe Photoshop®.

3. Share your designs as a PDF file. Click on the **Actions menu** and select **Share** from the popup window. Pick a preferred quality from Good, Better, and Best. Then, select a storage location. This format is ideal for distributing online.

4. Share your creative designs as a JPEG file. It is a Web-ready file format. Go to your screen and click on **Actions.** From the list, select the

Share icon and click on **JPEG.** Then, choose a location for your file storage. This format helps to flatten your artpiece into one layer and it is a lossy format.

5. Using the PNG file format. This format maintains transparency and offers a superior quality design. From the interface, click on **Actions** and select the **Share button.** Then, choose PNG from the options and tap a preferred storage location. It is a lossless format that can flatten your designs while maintaining its complete quality.

6. Sharing your artwork using a TIFF file. Simply, click on the **Actions menu** and choose the **Share button.** Then, click on **TIFF icon** from the list. This format helps to flatten the layers and preserves the quality of your image. Therefore, TIFF files are larger than other files.

How to Project your Canvas

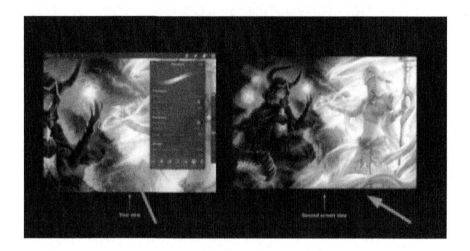

This is a setting located in the Actions menu. The Project canvas is under the **Prefs tab.** Most professionals call it the **AirPlay Canvas.** It is useful for showing your canvas on another monitor through AirPlay. It is connected with a cable making people to see what you are drawing properly.

It is only the canvas and your artwork that will be displayed on the second screen and not the contents on your gallery or interface.

CHAPTER SIX

Viewing and Handling Animation

Settings in Procreate

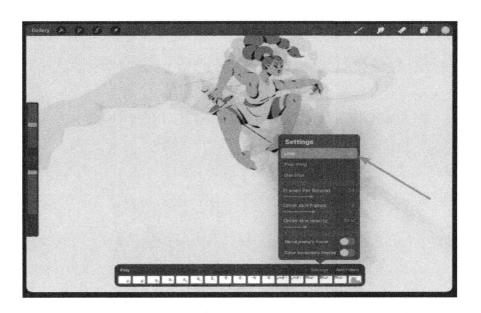

You can change the appearance, timing, and attributes of your animation. Change the speed and looping of your animation including the settings of onion skin.

Scroll to the right side of your **Animation Assist toolbar** and click on the **Settings menu.** This section handles the settings for the entire animation including the Animation Assist Interface.

You can go to the Frames options to choose the separate frames.

How to Handle the Animation Settings

a. Using the Frames per second method

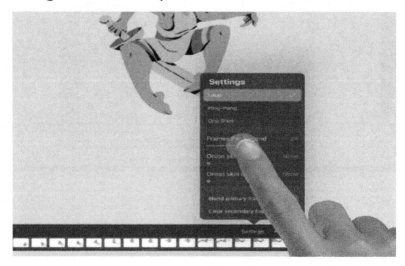

To change the speed of your animation, you can use the Frames per second (fps). Animation plays different drawings quickly as they tend to move. They play at 12 drawings per second. But cinematic animation is about 24 drawings per second. You will enjoy a smoother view if the frames per second is higher.

Frames per second can help in slowing down or speeding up existing animations in your system. Slow down the frame rate and slow down an animation. Also, you can add more frames in-between frames in your animation to slow it down.

Simply, pull the Frames per second timer and change the frame rate. Another way is setting it between one fps to sixty fps.

b. Using One Shot, Loop, or Ping Pong

You can set your animation to play on repeat loop, in a forward and reverse loop, or once. The switches on top of the Settings panel are designed to provide three different ways to handle your animation frames. These include loop, ping pong, and one shot.

In the loop setting, the frames can play from beginning to the end. It will loop backward, restart, and play till the end. The setting is continuous.

In the Ping Pong setting, the frames will play from beginning to the end. It will repeat the process again and again.

Also, in the one shot setup, the frames will play from the beginning to the end once and finish.

c. Using Onion Skinning

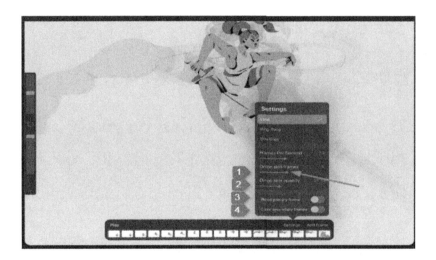

There are semi-transparent copies of drawings on the corner of your present frame. The sheets of animation paper are thin and light like onion skins; this art is known as onion-skinning. Traditionally, in hand drawn animation, the animators apply stack sheets of drawings on each other over a lightbox.

The light passing through the papers will highlight the drawings around the current one. With this, animators will understand what to draw again.

The various types of onion skins include onion skin frames, onion skin opacity, blend primary frame, and color primary frame.

Handling a Third-party Stylus

You can use third-party stylus on your iPad but the models of iPad not compatible with Apple Pencil are iPad mini 4, iPad Air 2, and 5th generation iPad.

The best stylus to use on Procreate is Apple Pencil. It is compatible with the models of iPad. Most third-party styli are not supported on iPad devices. But you need to do extensive research before you can locate the one that you can use on your system.

How to Pause a Frame

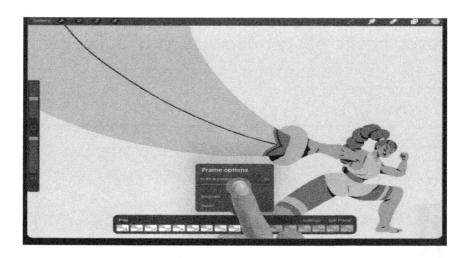

You can initiate a pause by changing a slider to hold a single drawing for various frames. This is done during animation and created by playing the same art design over different frames.

The pictures can stay paused the more if the frame holds last longer. Timing and rhythm could be adjusted using holds. You can pull the **Hold duration slider** to your desired number of frames up to a maximum of 120 frames.

If you want to remove a hold, simply drag the slider back to the **None position.** Moreover, the series of greyed-out frames are displayed on the Timeline.

Removing a Frame

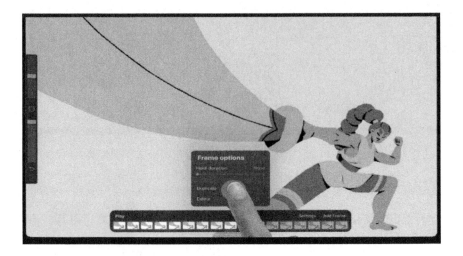

If you want to remove or delete a frame, tap and select it. Click on it again to launch the **Frame options.** Press on the **Delete icon** to get rid of the selected frame beside the Timeline.

What are Frame Options in Procreate?

Frame options are located in the animation Timeline. They involve duplicate, delete, and hold options.

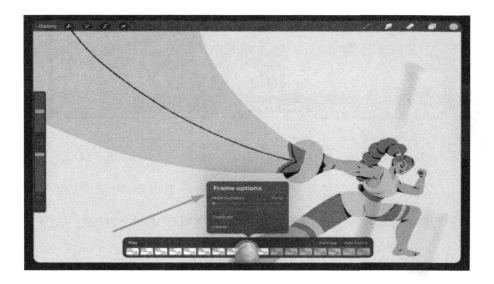

Simply, click on the Timeline to choose a frame. Click on the frame a second time to initiate the **Frame Options tab.** This bar controls the **Settings menu** that handles other frames in your animation.

You can decide to change settings for the entire animation and **Animation Assist Interface.**

Copying a Frame

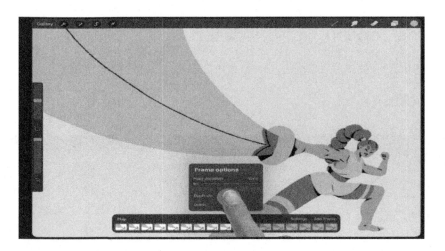

If you want to copy or duplicate a frame, select a frame by pressing on it. Press it again to launch the **Frame options.** Click on the **Duplicate icon** to make a replica of your chosen frame close to the Timeline. You can also get rid of a frame by clicking on the **Delete icon** if you want.

However, if you want to undo any option, use a two-finger tap.

Using Animation Timeline

The Animation Timeline is designed to help you know the visual timeline of your frames. Also, onion-skinning will help to track your progress with automatic playback and flexible settings.

Every frame of your animation is shown as a thumbnail. It is designed like the Layers palette but turned sideways. In the Layers panel, you will see the bottom layer in the extreme right of the Timeline. Therefore, the frames are organized chronologically beginning from the left to the right side.

Here are some of the ways to explore the Timeline:

1. Skip to a frame by tapping on it.
2. You can pull the timeline forward and backward.
3. Scroll through the timeline rapidly by flicking on it.
4. Any chosen frame will be underlined in blue color.

How to Share your Animation

If you want to export your animation as an animated MP4, GIF, or PNG, you should share the animation at the upper left of the interface. Click on the **Wrench button** representing the Actions icon. From the options, select the **Share button.**

Within this Share menu, you will see three formats for transferring animation to others. All the formats handle the animation differently.

a. Animated PNG – transfer all layers from your art designs to an animated PNG. You will enjoy a better visual quality than animated

GIFs. Simply, click on **Actions menu** and tap on the **Share icon**. From the options, choose **Animated PNG** and launch the interface. Also, you can choose either Web Ready or Max Resolution.

b. Animated MP4 – you can transfer all the layers of your artpiece to an animated MP4. These files use JPEG encoding for their frames without transparent backgrounds. They also have smaller size of file. Simply, click on the **Actions menu** and select **Share.** From the list, tap on **Animated MP4.** This will launch the **Animated MP4 Interface.** Select either **Max Resolution** or **Web Ready.** Max resolution has better quality with larger file size while Web ready has lower quality and smaller size of file. You can change the speed of your animation using Frames per second (fps).

c. Animated GIF – you can also transfer all your artwork to an animated GIF. Simply, click on the **Actions menu** and tap on **Share.** From the options, you can select Animated GIF. This will open the interface for Animated GIF. Then, select either Max Resolution or Web Ready.

Inserting Background to Animation

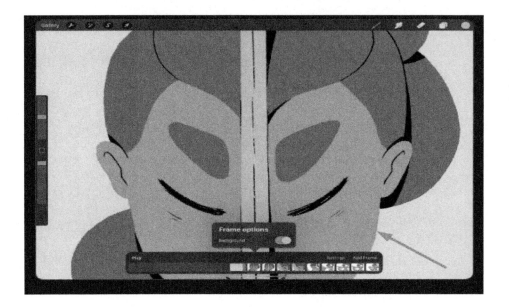

You can make a locked-in animation layer in the underlying background. This background locks a frame into a position as a constant background item. It will be displayed below other frames of your animation.

Scroll to the **Timeline** and click on the left frame to prompt the **Frame options.** Then, select the Background toggle. You can designate the frames on the left side as a Background and only one Background layer at a time.

Again, you can transfer any layer to the left side and set it as a Background layer. After this setup, every other layer will be displayed at the right side of the **Background frame.**

Here, the Background layer is locked in the lower position. It will not go over the layers.

Inserting Foreground to Animation

To insert a foreground to animation, create a locked-in floating foreground layer. It is designed to lock a frame into place making it a constant foreground item. It is displayed on the upper part of every other frame of your animation.

Scroll to the Timeline and click on the frame at the right side. This will prompt the Frame options. Then, press on the foreground toggle. The frame at the right hand can be designated as a Foreground and there is only a Foreground at a time.

Therefore, if you want to assign any frame as a Foreground, simply move it to the right side. If you make any other layer after this, they will be shown on the left side of the interface. Also, the contents of these frames are overlapped by the contents in the Foreground layer.

However, you can change a Foreground frame to a Background frame by pressing again on the **Foreground toggle.**

CHAPTER SEVEN

How to Customize the Time-Lapse

Settings

You can use the time-lapsed video to record your settings. It helps in recording every step of the creation of your pictures. After this, it compiles the record into a high-speed video replay. Therefore, you can share your creation with people.

When you create a new canvas, the time-lapse video will be enabled by default. On a good quality setting, your system can record the progress of your video at a resolution of 1080p. You cannot change the setting while you are recording but before you begin.

To customize the settings of your Procreate interface, follow these procedures:

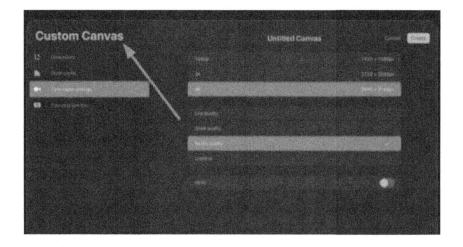

a. Go to the **Gallery** and hit the **Plus icon** on the upper right side of the window.

b. This will usher in the **New Canvas screen.**

c. Also, you will notice a small button with two rectangles that have a smaller **Plus icon**.

d. Click on this to reveal the **Custom Canvas menu**.

e. Then, press on the **Time-lapse settings**.

f. From this point, you can change the **Time-lapse section** of your new canvas.

g. Choose your video resolution from 1080p to full 4K.

h. Customize the settings of your recording quality from Low to Lossless.

You can use HEVC, which is a new type of video compression suitable for creating advanced motion graphics. It is usually off by default and can be toggled on. After all these procedures, click on the **Create button** to set it up.

How to Create a Time-Lapse Video

A Time-lapsed video is used for recording every procedure during the making of your artwork. It is then complied into a high=speed video replay. You can transfer and share this recording with the world.

Whenever you create a new canvas, Time-lapse video is enabled by default. It can record your speed at a resolution of 1080p. This is on a good quality setting that cannot be altered during recording but you must set up the features before you start recording your artwork.

Deactivating Time-lapse Videos

You can disable recording Time-lapse videos completely. This is a default setting in Procreate. If you use the toggle in **Actions menu,** it stops the recording feature in your present canvas. But recording may proceed on other canvasses including new ones.

You can deactivate recording completely on all canvasses including present and future ones by clicking on **Help menu** and selecting **Advanced Setting.** At this stage, you will go out of Procreate into the iPad settings. From the options, select the **Procreate menu.** Then, toggle the **Disable time-lapse button on.**

This action turns off Time-lapse by default on all the files from that moment onwards. Even, on new canvasses, it will not be activated and recording will also cease. You won't be able to retrieve a recording after disabling the Time-lapse feature.

If you want to reactivate it, follow the procedures above and it will start working.

Reviewing Time-Lapse Videos

It is possible to preview your Time-lapse video without leaving the Procreate app. Scroll to the **Actions menu** and select **Video.** From the options on the screen, tap on the **Time-lapse Replay icon.**

With this, the video in Procreate is replayed on a loop at thirty fps. You can determine the video runtime using the counter on the screen. You can flip forward and backward through the replay by dragging your finger to the right side or left side across the canvas.

Pinch zoom and go around the canvas when the video is playing. In this way, you can concentrate on the details. If you want to replay and return to your art design, press the **Done icon.**

Sharing Time-lapse Videos

To share your time-lapse video, click on **Actions** and choose **Video.** Then, from the menu, press on **Export Time-lapse video.**

Now, select between thirty seconds and full length. The full length is made to export your entire creation using a high-speed video. It will last throughout the process in a considerable length.

However, the thirty seconds recording removes frames from the video and this process speeds up the recording. There is an algorithm that maintains the most necessary details in the video. The highest amount of frames is preserved during the making of the artwork. At this stage, the frames are constantly changing.

But you can share your recording to any app attached to the interface of your Procreate app.

How to Adjust the Preferences

You can customize your preferences on Procreate to fit your workflow. Mirror your canvas to a connected window or adjust the look of your interface. Also, connect a third-party stylus and change the Pressure curve. Also, you can personalize the Gesture controls to adapt to the work you are doing.

Move to the **Actions menu** and select **Prefs.** This will change the appearance and feel of your interface. You can do this with sliders and toggles. Some of these toggles include

a. Using the Dark or light interface – you will find two visual modes on the interface. These include the dark mode or light mode. The dark mode is a charcoal like platform that enables you to maintain focus on your creativity. Also, the light mode is designed for greater contrast and enables you to handle your projects in brighter conditions.

b. Working on the Right-hand or left-hand interface – the sidebar is located on the left side of the window. Toggle the button on the right-hand interface if you want to move the sidebar to the right.

c. Working with Brush cursor – the outlines of the shape of your brush will show if you activate the **Brush cursor** and simply tap your canvas. With this, you can see the type of shape you can make.

d. Using Project canvas – toggle project canvas after connecting a second screen with an AirPlay or cable. The second window will show only the full-screen canvas with no zoom, interface, and other distractions. With this, you can concentrate on the details of your project while maintaining the final outcome of your designs.

e. Using rapid Undo delay – this is one of the shortcuts in Procreate. It features a two-finger hold for rapid Undo. Press your two fingers on the canvas. After a short delay, Procreate will move rapidly through Undo procedures. Now, you can remove unwanted strokes on your work. You can use the slider to set the Rapid Undo effect, which could be some seconds.

f. Applying Selection mask visibility – after initiating a selection, it will change to a selection mask. With this, you can know the areas of the canvas that are masked but not selected. If you see areas that appear semi-transparent by default with shifting diagonal shading, they are masked areas. Simply, change the Selection mask visibility slider to adjust the transparency. With this, your changes could become more or less pronounced. The changes you have made will appear shortly.

CHAPTER EIGHT

What is a Drawing Guide?

The Drawing Guide in Procreate involves four different methods, which are 2D grid, Symmetry, Perspective, and Isometric. It is located at the upper left in the Wrench menu with open canvas.

Click on the **Wrench bar** to launch the Actions menu. Click on the **Canvas bar** and select **Drawing Guide** to enable the tool. From the menu, press on the **Edit Drawing Guide** to open the interface of the Drawing Guide.

How to Customize a Guide

To customize your guide, navigate to the lower toolbar and apply the Opacity or Thickness sliders. Also, use the Hue slider located on the upper toolbar to customize the appearance of your guide lines.

However, you can alter the position of your guide lines with the blue bode. You can also use the green node to rotate the guides.

How to Rotate a Guide

You can design a grid with perfect sizes for your artwork. You can customize the spacing of guidelines with the Grid Size slider. Another way is pressing on the measurement readout to input the real value in centimeters, millimeters, inches, and pixels.

Apply these settings together with the custom canvas design to make artworks that are perfect for printing.

How to Enable a Guide

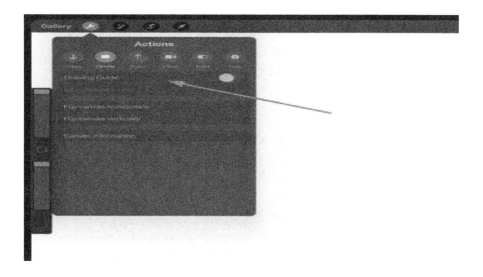

If you want to enable a guide, move to your **Actions menu** and you will locate options to toggle and edit the **Drawing Guide** for a particular art design. But if you have not used a Drawing Guide on your canvas, you will need to enable it using the switch. Then, click on **Edit Drawing Guide menu.**

How to Position Guides

You can position your Drawing Guides by choosing from four formats. These include Symmetry, Isometric, perspective, and 2D grid guides.

Scroll to the toolbar and select the button you want. This will enable you to adjust to a preferred guide. But the lower toolbar is designed for customizing the guide lines. By selecting a mode, the default guide lines will be displayed automatically in position. Then, you can change or customize them the way you want.

You can create up to three vanishing points if you select the perspective mode for your work.

Using the Symmetry Guide

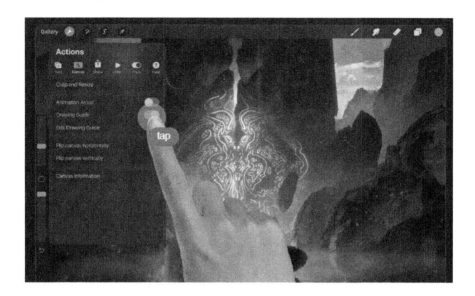

To inject a mind-bending effect into your artwork, use the symmetry guide. Then, you should set up and customize the symmetry guide.

Navigate to the **Actions menu** and select **Canvas.** From the options, you should click on **Edit Drawing Guide.** This will redirect you to the **Drawing Guides menu.**

The Vertical Symmetry Guide is displayed by default. This is shown as thin lines overlaying your creative designs.

But you can customize the appearance of the guide using these procedures:

1. Horizontal symmetry features – there is a guideline over the center of your canvas causing your drawings on the upper part to be replicated in the bottom half. Also, whatever you draw on the lower part will be reproduced on top.

2. Vertical symmetry features – you will see a guideline vertically down in the center of the canvas. This will cause whatever you draw to be shown on the other side of the screen. You can induce mirrored effects on a point by rotating this guide.

3. Rotation and Position features – pull both nodes to change the real positions of the grid lines. This blue positional node transfers the entire grid to the canvas. The green rotational node turns over the grid lines. But you can reset the grid to the default position by pressing any of the nodes. Then, select the **Reset button.**

4. Radial symmetry features – this feature divides your canvas into eight different segments with vertical, diagonal, or horizontal guide lines. That means whatever you draw in a segment will be replicated in others naturally.

5. Mirrored vs Rotational features – new symmetry guides use mirror symmetry reflecting your strokes across the guideline. Therefore, in rotational symmetry mode, the stroke is shown and rotated. But the reproduction is flipped either vertically or horizontally. Simply, click on the Rotational Symmetry switch to move between both effects.

6. Using the Cancel or Commit feature – if you don't want to make any change and return to the canvas, click on the **Cancel icon.** But to effect changes on your canvas, press on **Done.**

7. The Appearance of the Drawing Guide - the appearance of your drawing guide is affected by adjusting the color of the guide lines. The color tab is located over the **Drawing Guides**

menu. You can also change the transparency of the guide lines from unseen to seen.

Another way is using the Assisted Drawing to change the strokes instantly and match the direction of the guidelines. This is activated by default in symmetry mode.

8. Quadrant Symmetry features – this feature shares the canvas into quadrants with a vertical and horizontal guideline. There will be a replica of your creations in one quadrant on all others.

How to Apply Perspective Guides

If you want to set up adjustable vanishing points, you can use the perspective guides. You can use these features to create realistic backgrounds and items in your art piece.

To set up the perspective guide, navigate to the Actions screen and locate the Canvas tab. From the options, select **Edit Drawing Guide.** You will be directed to the **Drawing Guides window.**

Go to the lower part of the screen and select the **Perspective icon.** This will show as thin lines overlaying your artwork. To change the appearance of your guide, use the following options:

1. Appearance – here, you can change the color of the guide line with the hue bar located at the upper part of the **Drawing Guides area.** The thickness of the guidelines could be changed from invisible to visible. Also, the transparency of the guide lines could be changed from unseen to opaque. On the

other hand, you can instantly change your strokes to match the direction of the guide lines using the **Drawing Assist.**

2. Apply Commit or Cancel – to set up any change you have made already, click on the **Done icon.** But to return to the Canvas menu without making changes, click on **Cancel.**

3. Use Position and rotation features - you can change the range and position of your grid lines by pulling the blue nodes and horizon line.

4. Use One-Point Perspective feature – the easiest type of perspective, whereby all the surfaces in the images facing you appear as the real shape. It does not have distortion. The vertical lines and horizontal lines become parallel with the edges of the canvas including the horizon of the art design. This feature is also known as parallel perspective. In this instance, only the areas moving away or towards the viewer will be distorted. These lines will meet at a vanishing point.

5. Inserting Vanishing Points – simply, click any point on the screen to make a vanishing point. There could be up to three vanishing points to allow for one-point perspective, two-point perspective, and three-point perspective.

6. Removing vanishing points – you can remove a vanishing point from your artwork by clicking on the **Delete button** to remove it.

7. Two-perspective – in this perspective, only two vertical lines are parallel. But every horizontal line meets at any of the two points on the horizon line. You will have a better realistic effect than one-point perspective.

8. Three-point perspective - all lines recede towards one of the three vanishing points. It is just like the way we visualize in reality. This feature impresses believable height, depth, and width.

Using the Isometric Guide

If you want to add a third dimension to your drawings, you should use isometric guides. It is suitable for technical drawings, engineering, and other architectural designs.

The first approach is to set up and customize the guide. Scroll to the **Actions menu** and click on **Canvas**. From the options, tap on **Edit Drawing guide** and you will be redirected to the **Drawing Guides** menu.

Then, press the isometric icon on the upper part of the window. This is shown as thin lines overlaying your artwork. But you can change the appearance and features of the isometric guide in the following ways:

1. Appearance option – you can change the color of the guide lines with the hue bar at the upper part of the **Drawing Guides menu.** You can also change the transparency of the guide lines from invisible to opaque. Another way is to adjust the thickness of the guide lines from unseen to seen. You can also change the grid size by adjusting the scale of the grid. Finally, you can employ the Drawing Assist to match the direction of the guide lines and adjust your strokes automatically.

2. Commit or Cancel option – after making your changes, you can commit them by clicking on **Done.** Also, if you want to undo the changes you have made and return to the canvas, click on the **Cancel button.**

3. Rotation and position features – you can change the position of your grid lines by dragging both nodes. To move the entire grid above the canvas, use the blue positional node. Also, to rotate the grid lines, use the green rotational node.

You can reset the grid to its default position by clicking one of the nodes. Then, select the **Reset icon.**

CHAPTER NINE

Using the 2D Grid

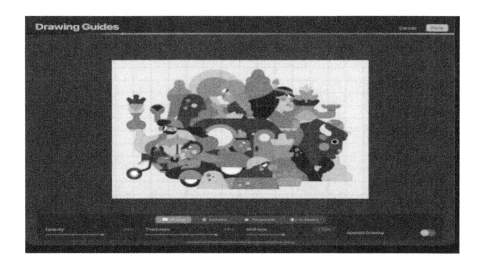

To maintain your artworks in proportion, apply 2D grids. It is required for designing two-dimensional shapes. If you enable Drawing Assist, you can use 2D grids to maintain your strokes.

If you want to set up and adjust 2D grids, scroll to the **Actions menu** and tap on **Canvas.** Press on the

Edit Drawing Guide. You will be redirected to the **Drawing Guides window.**

Go to the lower part of the window and select 2D grid button. Then, you will see 2D grid displayed as thin lines overlaying your artwork.

Now, to customize your guide, follow these procedures:

a. Use Rotation or Position method – change the real positions of the grid lines by pulling the two nodes. The entire grid will be transferred over the canvas using the blue positional node. Also, the green rotational node rotates over the grid lines. If you want to reset the grid to the default position, click on one of the nodes and select the **Reset icon.**

b. Use the Appearance method – this includes adjusting the color of the guide lines with the hue bar at the upper part of the **Drawing Guides window.** You can also adjust the transparency of the guide lines from hidden to expose. Another way is to change the thickness of the guide lines from unseen to seen. Then, you can adjust the scale of the grid using Drawing Assist. This automatically changes your stokes to align with the direction of the guidelines.

c. Use the Cancel or Commit menu. To return to the canvas without altering your details, click on **Cancel**. But to apply the changes you have made, press **Done.**

Handling the Drawing Assist

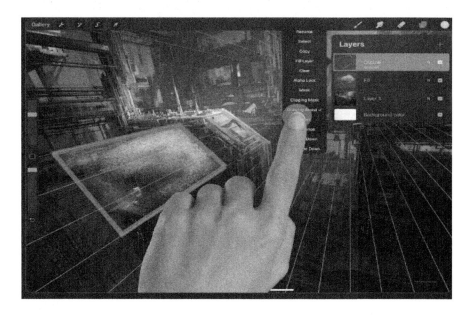

After selecting a Drawing Guide, the Drawing Assist links your strokes to the Drawing Guide enabling to have perfect drawings. It aligns the marks you make on the canvas to the Drawing Guide by acting like an unseen ruler in the app.

You can enable it on the Drawing Guides screen by toggling Assisted Drawing on to activate it in your original layer. After activation, an Assisted label will display on that layer within the **Layers panel**.

Then, if you set up a Symmetry guide the Drawing Assist will activate by default.

Another way to activate Drawing Assist is through **Layer Options menu.** To make the Layer Options popup, press on the primary layer once. From the list, select **Drawing Assist.** If you enable Drawing Assist through the Layer Options area, it prompts up the last Drawing Guide you applied on your present canvas including your previous settings.

You can use freehand drawing on the canvas but ensure that you deactivate Drawing Assist. Also, you should draw on a normal layer below or above the Assisted layer area.

How to Draw with QuickShape

QuickShape is designed to take hand-drawn lines and shapes and change them into perfect shapes instantly. Make a drawing and place your finger on the canvas.

Immediately, QuickShape will appear and transform such drawings or marks into neat forms.

141

After making the shape, continue pressing it down and place another finger on the canvas. With this action, a square can change into a rectangle while a circle will change to an oval.

Now, if you want to scale and rotate the shape you made, continue placing your hand on the canvas. Drag and change the scale and rotation of your shape or line.

You can also rotate your shape in incremental form by placing another finger on the canvas while pulling your shape. With this, you can rotate your shape in 15 degrees increments.

To edit QuickShape, tap on the Edit Shape icon in the notification menu at the upper side of the canvas.

Using Freehand Drawing

You can polish your creative designs using the intuitive selective method based on hand drawing. Click on the polygonal lines and draw to initiate a freehand selection. You can handle complex diagrams by using either the freehand method or polygonal lines method.

Simply, press the Selection icon to display the Selection toolbar. From the options, you should click on **Freehand.** The freehand drawing could be made using a pencil or finger.

If you want to zoom, use Procreates navigation gestures. Also, you can pan and flip your canvas in the **Selection menu.**

To create polygonal selections, click on the canvas to position corner nodes linked by straight lines. Press your finger or pencil on the canvas at the point where you want to place a corner node.

Insert more corner nodes as you press around the canvas. All the dashed lines will be linked to the nodes with a straight line from the existing node.

After this, click on the starting point and the origin of your line will show a gray circle. Click on this to end the selection. You can still insert more areas to the selection. On the other hand, you can pick a tool and start editing.

Press the Add or Remove icons. You can add the selection and ensure the selection mode is active for future modifications.

Click on any tool and start editing if you are satisfied with your drawing. The selection will be committed if you notice a semi-transparent moving diagonal line or lines outside the selected sections on the canvas.

Applying Automatic Drawing

Automatic drawing enables you to choose areas of your artwork with one touch. Press on the **Selection icon** to initiate the Selection toolbar. From the menu, you can click on **Automatic button.**

When you click other areas on your canvas, the Automatic mode will insert them into your selection.

What are vanishing Points in Procreate?

Vanishing points are peculiar spots on the horizontal lines. It occurs when two or more lines meet at a point in the distance and become one, two, or more vanishing points.

How to Import Images

To import images, go to the **Files app** and make a new canvas. You can also drag and drop a picture inside Procreate.

Another method is to import from files. Click on the Import icon in the upper right of the Gallery menu. This will open the **Files app.** Then, press onto a file to pick it up and drag it into Procreate.

You can also transfer files from photos by dragging and dropping them into the canvas.

How to Paint Images

You can paint pictures by inking, shading, sketching, texturing, and painting in different ways. Add colors to your designs through painting.

You can click on the Brush tool to pick a brush from the library. Make strokes by tapping your finger on the canvas. Apply both sliders in the sidebar on the left. This will adjust transparency and size of your brush strokes.

Navigate the Brush library and see several peculiar brushes. This will show you different effects beginning from realistic to exciting features.

You can also change the settings of existing brushes. Another way is going to the Brush Studio and building your own personal brush.

Painting with Apple Pencil

Another important way to paint images is using an Apple Pencil. This will help you to unlock the full potentials of Procreate app. With this, your designs will appear as if you are using a natural pencil. You can change the appearance of your brush strokes using pressure and tilt. This will change the thickness, scatter, darkness, and opacity of your images. Even the strokes you make could be changed.

How to Smudge Images

If you want to blend your creativity, combine colors, and straighten or smoothen marks and strokes on your drawings, tap on the **Smudge icon.** It is necessary to transfer colors around your canvas.

Click on the **Smudge menu** and pick a brush from the library. Click or pull your finger on the colors and brushstrokes. This will blend your work.

You will experience different effects based on the degree of the opacity slider. Make the smudge more pronounced by increasing the opacity slider within the sidebar. You can also reduce the opacity to get a cooler effect.

Erasing Photos

To erase images in Procreate app, go to the gallery and swipe to the left side on the photo. You will see a menu with options to **Delete, Duplicate, or Share.** Tap on the **Delete icon.**

Another way is to swipe right and the Share Arrow including a Trash Basket will show. Tap on the Trash basket to remove the image.

CHAPTER TEN

Setting Up Brushes in Procreate

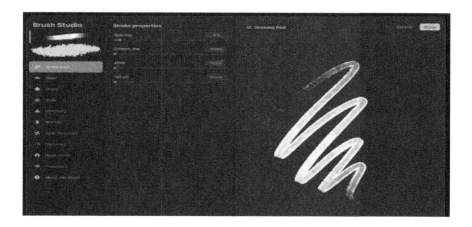

To set up brushes in Procreate, you need to discover various settings and the features of each of them.

1. Rendering – you can render the brush to the screen in many ways. This is changing render modes under the hood. You should customize

the behavior of strokes and colors on your brush as they make contact with the canvas.

2. Stroke Path – makes strokes by plotting several points along the path your Apple pencil or finger makes across the canvas. Some of the properties of Stroke include jitter, spacing, fall off, and streamline.

3. Shape – transfer an image into the shape source by adjusting the shape of a brush tip. Therefore, you can change the scatter, frequency, width, and rotation including other aspects of the shape.

4. Dynamics – you can set your brush to effect dynamic changes depending on how you make strokes. Add unpredictability to a brush by casually setting the opacity and jitter size of the brush.

5. Grain – use the Grain editor to design a new grain from any image. You can determine if the grain remains behind your strokes or follows them. With this feature, you can customize depth, scale, and blend mode.

6. Color Dynamics – you should maximize the potentials of digital art by setting your Procreate brush to change brightness, saturation, and color depending on the degree of tilt and pressure applied to the Apple pencil. If you select a secondary color, you can move between secondary and primary colors. All these are applied as individual settings. They can be used in a combination and you can handle the colors in different ways.

7. Taper – customizes the thickness and opacity of your brush making the tapered side function naturally.

Different Types of Brushes

As an illustrator or a hobbyist trying to exploit the creativities in Procreate, here are various brushes that you can use for your artworks. These include watercolor brushes, hair and fur brushes, manga and anime brushes, acrylic brushes, ink brushes, texture brushes, oil brushes, blacklettter brushes, acrylic brushes, lettering brushes, etc.

Navigating the Brush Studio

The Brush studio is made to ensure the uniqueness of individual brushes. It has various customization features. You can use the settings in the Brush Studio to manage the brushes by tweaking the basics and diving deeper for a greater range of effects.

There are two procedures to explore the versatility of the Brush studio.

a. Move into the studio and adjust the settings before you start creating your designs.
b. You can test and experiment with the various brushes to create a nice object for yourself.

If you want to enter the Brush studio, press on the Plus (+) button on the upper right side. Also, you can tap on the **Brush icon** to launch the **Brush library.**

The Brush Studio Interface

This interface consists of three sides such as Attributes, Settings, and Drawing pad.

The attributes consists of eleven items with different settings that you can modify to suit your drawings. They are located in the left menu bar.

The settings enable you to insert various features in the settings using toggles, simple controls, and sliders. There are customizable settings in the left menu of the app for you.

The drawing pad is made to enable you preview your brushes before applying them on your canvas. It is useful for testing colors.

Managing the Brush Library

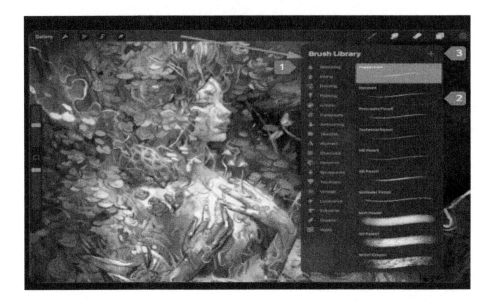

There are various brushes built-into Procreate. These brushes are arranged into themed categories with hundreds of brushes in the Brush library. With these tools, you can continue on endless experimentation of your artistic creations.

To initiate the **Brush library**, locate the **Brush icon** shaped like a paintbrush on the right menu bar of the interface Procreate. Press the Brush tool once and enable it. Then, click on it again to prompt the Brush Library.

Zooming in and Out in Procreate

From experience, zooming in or out of Procreate is usually difficult. Most times, the image is frozen and unable to move.

Rectangle and Eclipse Drawing

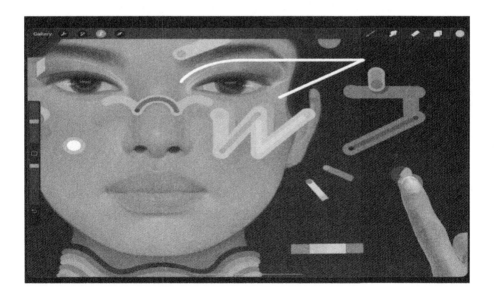

If you want simple tools for your selection, you will see them in Procreate. To make an elliptical or rectangular selection, pull a shape into position.

Launch the Selection toolbar by clicking on the **Selection icon.** From the options, click on the **Ellipse or Rectangle button.** You can pull your favorite shape over the content you want to select.

You can modify your selection using the available tools. Use the Add or Remove buttons to apply the selections you made and keep them activated for your projects.

Freeform Transform

This is useful for scaling and rotating content. Press and pull the layer with a finger after enabling the Transform mode. Simply, press any part of the canvas either inside or outside the bounding box. This will enable you to shift the image or content.

Uniform Transform

There are two methods of transforming an image under the uniform mode. The uniform mode transforms but maintains the original proportions of the object. You can use Quick Scale to transform contents from the middle by pinching inside the box. This will enable you to scale the content with the image anchoring at the center of the bounding box. Then, it can increase or reduce from that point.

Managing Distortions and Warping

Distortions

Distortion in Procreate produces angled effects, tilt effects, and 3D effects. Use a finger to move the selection or layer after enabling Transform. Simply, tap and pull anywhere on the canvas. It could be outside or inside the bounding box.

This feature enables you to paint an image as if you are looking at it straight ahead. You can imitate a three-dimensional area by distorting the image into a receding angle. Simply, click on the **Distort icon** in the Transform toolbar. Pull any corner node to start your Transformation.

Another way to distort an object in Procreate is using Shear. You can use it to angle an object and make the appearance of depth.

Warping

Warping in Procreate occurs when you fold and wrap your art designs in unpredictable magnitudes using the Warp mesh. Go to the Transform toolbar and press the Warp icon. You will see it in a box with solid edges rather than moving dashes.

Open the box; you will see a grid overlaying your content like a mesh. Simply, pull the sides, edges, and inner mesh to warp any corner of the content as you like.

You can use advanced mesh and node control in the Transform menu to wrap your contents.

CHAPTER ELEVEN

Understanding Layers

In Procreate, layers are used for layering various contents on each other. Despite this interaction, they also maintain a form of individuality.

You can group the layers if you are handling complex tasks. It is useful for tidying up the interface. Again, you can locate any layer quickly if you want to edit it.

We also have reference layer in Procreate. This is an advanced feature enabling you to maintain your work intact as you color it on a different layer. Another aspect of layers to know is the combination of layers.

This involves merging layers by scrolling to the **Layers menu** and pressing on a layer. This will prompt **Layer**

options. From the list, you should tap on **Merge Down.** You can merge multiple groups of layers with a pinch of your fingers.

Pinch the upper and lower layers you want to merge. They will merge together.

Creating Layers

To create a new layer, go to a **New document** by default. You will see two layers such as Layer 1 and Background color. Any layer you selected will be displayed in blue. You can create a new layer by pressing the **Plus icon** in your **Layers menu.** Then, a new layer pops up over an active layer.

By creating new layers, you can place each element on a separate layer. You can rename or customize the names of your layers for clarity.

You can enhance transparency by turning off the background. This will help you in building a background color of your choice. After creating your art designs, you can add colors since the layer of the background color is white by default.

Go to the Layers panel and click on a **Background Color layer.** This will prompt the Color Panel where you will choose a new color for the background of your creative designs. After the set up, click on **Done** and leave the **Color Panel.**

Various layer Options

The Layer options provide different ways of interacting with the layers in a single touch.

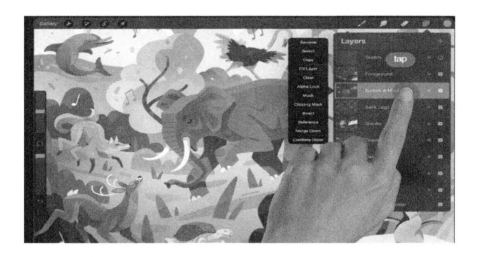

Go to the Layers panel and click on a layer once to select it. Then, click it again to access the Layers menu.

Here are some of the various layer options in Procreate:

a. Rename the layer – this is used to give your layer a custom name. They are numbered by default such as Layer 1, Layer 2, etc. Go to the

Layer options and click on Rename. After renaming your layer, click on Return or tap anywhere on the canvas to dismiss the keyboard.

b. Choose the contents of a layer. Go to the Layers panel and click on a layer to prompt the **Layer options**. Then, click on the **Select icon**.

c. Copy the active layer to the clipboard – this will bring up the Layer options. Then, select the **Copy icon.**

d. Use a flat color to fill a layer. Scroll to the **Layers menu** and click a layer. With this, the entire layer will be filled with the chosen color.

e. Clear options – this will enable you to clear an entire layer automatically. Go to the **Layer menu** and select a layer to bring up **Layer Options**. Then, click on the **Clear icon.**

Opacity in Procreate Layers

To manage layer opacity in the Layers menu, click with two fingers on the layer you want to change opacity. The menu closes and you can slide your fingers or pen at any point to adjust its opacity.

The Blending Modes of layers

The contents in a layer maintain opacity by default and cover the contents of other layers below it. However, two layers can interact together with their objects and colors. You can preview all your options on the interface quickly using the Blend modes.

You can change these modes by opening the Layers panel and clicking the double rectangle icon located in the upper right side of the window.

You will see some letters displayed on the right side of each layer. This will inform you of the Blend Mode that is activated. There are two parts of Blend Modes the current blend mode and opacity.

Types of Blend modes

The various types of blend modes include linear burn, darken, color burn, darker color, multiply, darker value, screen, lighten, color dodge, light color, overlay, add, hard light, hard light, soft light, pin light, hard mix, etc.

How to Organize Layers

There are various controls in Procreate that you can use in organizing your system. These controls include moving, locking, duplicating, and deleting of layers.

Here are different ways to organize your layers:

a. Selection of Layers – control and edit various layers at once. You can do bulk moving, grouping, deletion, or even transformation. There are primary and secondary selections of layers for better control. To use the primary layers, click on any layer to turn it to an active layer. It will show in the Layers panel as bright blue. Swipe to the right on any layer and add it to your selection to make the secondary layer.

b. Combination of layers – you can combine multiple layers into Groups as this will keep your work tidy. After selecting multiple layers, the Group option will display at the upper right of the Layers panel. Press on it and all selected layers will be grouped.

c. Transferring layers using drag and drop - this will help you to reorganize all elements inside your canvas.

d. Transferring Layers and Layer Groups – press down a layer or Layer group to pick it. After this, pull it up or down in order and release it.

e. Transferring Primary and secondary layers – this action will move all selected secondary layers.

f. Transferring layers between canvasses – pressing and pulling layers from a canvas to another. Also, drop them in the gallery to make new canvasses.

Sharing Layers

Sharing layers enables you to transfer them from one artwork to a multi-page PDF, an MP4, an animated GIF, or a folder of PNGs.

Press Actions and select the **Share icon**. Go to Share Layers area of the Share bar and locate various layer export formats. In this case, only noticeable layers are exported or shared.

CONCLUSION

Are you an illustrator, graphics artist, or a creative designer interested in improving your skills? This book is written to enlighten you on the various ways the Procreate app in your iPad can bring a turnaround in your creativity and enhance your dexterity immensely.

If you have studied this book meditatively, nothing can stop you from maximizing your potentials in graphic designs. Even as a beginner, you have a book with vivid illustrations and texts written without ambiguity.

It forms the basics of your quest for mastery in using Procreate for your artwork projects. This will give you speed and more opportunities to experiment with a unique software.

ABOUT THE AUTHOR

Christopher Parker is an experienced graphics designer that has been using different tools such as Photoshop in creating high-quality designs. He offers tutorials and seminars on how a creative designer can use digital tools in handling their artworks. He studied Fine and Applied Arts from the University of Michigan. He is a researcher and a consultant.

Printed in Great Britain
by Amazon

38964561R00106